Wind socks are colorful displays in windy weather

#

Jennifer Fandel

A⁺

Smart Apple Media

COPYRIGHT

Published by Smart Apple Media

1980 Lookout Drive, North Mankato, MN 56003

Designed by Rita Marshall

Copyright © 2003 Smart Apple Media. International copyright reserved in all countries. No part of this book may be reproduced in any form without written permission from the publisher.

Printed in the United States of America

Photographs by CLEO Photography, JLM Visuals (Richard P. Jacobs), KAC Productions (Larry Ditto), Tom Myers, Tom Stack & Associates (Dr. Scott Norquay, Brian Parker, Inga Spence)

Library of Congress Cataloging-in-Publication Data

Fandel, Jennifer. Wind / by Jennifer Fandel. p. cm. — (Weather)

Includes bibliographical references and index.

Summary: Describes the formation, movement, and effects of wind, as well as presenting information on how meteorologists study them. Includes a simple experiment on air pressure.

ISBN 1-58340-153-9

1. Winds—Juvenile literature. [1. Winds.] I. Title. II. Weather (Smart Apple Media).

QC931.4 .F36 2002   551.51'8–dc21   2001049978

First Edition 9 8 7 6 5 4 3 2 1

Wind

CONTENTS

What Is Wind?

It shakes the leaves of the trees. It keeps kites flying high and helps sailboats travel. On a hot day, wind makes people feel cooler and more comfortable. Wind scatters seeds, causing new plants to grow. Strong wind can also carry soil away from farmers' fields. Wind sometimes reaches high speeds and causes great destruction, damaging everything from city buildings to entire forests. Wind is a very important part of the weather, and its effects—both good and bad—are everywhere.

Wind is caused by a surprising source: the sun. Because

of the earth's tilt, different parts of the earth receive different

amounts of sunlight. The sun shines most directly on the

equator, the middle of the earth, so places along the equator

People have invented many ways to ride the wind

receive the most heat. The North and South Poles receive the

least heat. These unbalanced temperatures cause uneven air

pressure. Warm air is light, so it rises and **expands**. It pushes

aside cooler air, which grows heavier, **contracts**, and sinks. The earth tries to balance the differences in temperature and air pressure by the constant movement of air. This movement creates wind.

Chicago, Illinois, is nicknamed "The Windy City" because of the strong winds that blow there.

Wind often signals changes in the weather

Windmills use wind to create electricity

How Wind Moves

There are two main types of wind **circulation**. The first type, known as global wind, moves in predictable patterns high above the earth. In general, cool air **Wind can make cold temperatures feel even colder. This effect is called windchill.** travels to the equator, while warm air travels to the poles. Because the earth spins so fast on its axis, however, the rotation causes global wind to move in horizontal bands. The direction of a wind depends on where it is located. Winds directly north and

Wind can push sailboats 50 miles (80 km) an hour

south of the equator are called trade winds, and they move to

the northwest. Winds around the North and South Poles are

called polar easterlies, and winds in between the equator and

the poles are called westerlies. Winds **The highest wind**
speed ever recorded
are named by where they start, so a **was 231 miles**
(372 km) per
westerly wind moves from west to **hour at Mount**
Washington, New
east, and an easterly wind moves from **Hampshire, in 1934.**

east to west. Local wind is the second type of wind

circulation. These winds move in patterns that are specific to

certain regions. Mountains, valleys, coasts, and other large land

forms may cause winds to act differently. In the Rocky

Mountains of Canada and the United States, for example,

winds called chinooks bring warm, dry weather to melt

Tree leaves can show the wind's direction and speed

the snow. The *mistral* is a strong, cold wind that blows along the coast of France. In North Africa, a local wind called a *haboob* creates violent sandstorms.

Keeping Track of Wind

Changes in the weather are often signaled by a shift in the wind, so people who are concerned with weather watch wind carefully. **Meteorologists** include information about wind speed and wind direction in their weather reports. Wind speed is measured with an instrument called an anemometer (an-eh-MOM-i-tur). Wind direction can be determined with

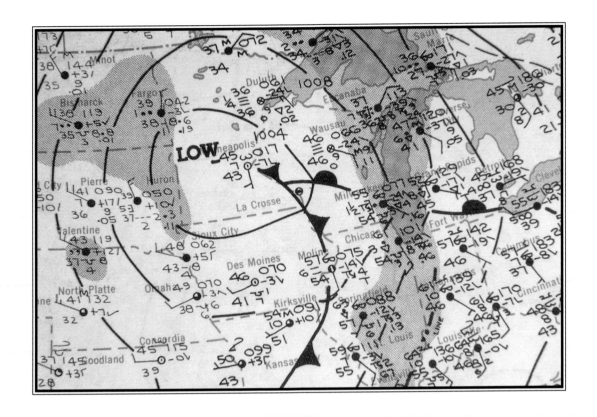

weather vanes or wind socks that point in the direction of the

wind. ⌁ People whose jobs depend on the weather, such

as farmers and airplane pilots, may watch for signs of their

Weather maps record information about wind patterns

own. The movement of flags, tree branches, and leaves can show the wind's direction and speed. Wind speed can also be determined using the Beaufort Scale, which estimates speed by charting the movements of trees, smoke, and bodies of water. The Beaufort Scale helps people determine if the wind is breezy, gusty, or downright dangerous.

Blowing in the Wind

Farmers are concerned about wind because strong wind can destroy crops and cause **erosion**. Farmers often plant rows of trees called windbreaks to slow the harmful effects of

wind. The erosion that wind can cause is also a concern for

people who work to preserve fragile areas, such as newly-

planted prairies. ∿ Spinning columns of air called

Rows of trees called windbreaks help protect crops

tornadoes are the fastest, most dangerous winds on Earth.

They can lift and throw cars, trains, and even houses! Nothing

can stop wind from blowing, so it is important to stay safe

and seek shelter when strong winds **Some ancient cultures believed that the wind was a messenger bringing good or bad news, depending on the wind's direction.** develop. Nevertheless, we should enjoy and be thankful for all the good things wind does. Whether it is seeds, air-

planes, or a kite, there is bound to be something riding

the wind.

Tornadoes over lakes or oceans are called waterspouts

Understanding Air Pressure

Air is always moving, creating wind. It moves in different ways depending on the temperature. You can see this for yourself by doing the following experiment.

What You Need

A large balloon
A plastic bottle (any size)
Hot and cold tap water

What You Do

1. Stretch the balloon over the neck of the bottle.
2. Place the bottom half of the bottle in hot water. Hold it in the water for 5 to 10 minutes.
3. Now put the bottom half of the bottle into cold water. Let the bottle stand in the water for 5 to 10 minutes.

What You See

When you put the bottle in hot water, the balloon should inflate. But when you set the bottle in cold water, the balloon should deflate. Warm air inside the bottle rises and expands, filling the balloon. Once the air cools, it sinks and contracts, deflating the balloon.

The movement of hot air makes these balloons float

Index

Words to Know

air pressure (AIR PREH-shur)—a downward force from the weight of air

circulation (sir-kyoo-LAY-shun)—continuous movement

contracts (kun-TRAKTS)—becomes larger

erosion (ee-RO-zhun)—the wearing away of land by wind or water

expands (ek-SPANDZ)—becomes smaller

meteorologists (mee-tee-or-ALL-o-jists)—scientists who study the weather

Read More

Elsom, Derek. *Weather Explained: A Beginner's Guide to the Elements.* New York: Henry Holt, 1997.

Haslam, Andrew, and Barbara Taylor. *Weather.* Chicago: World Book Publishing, 1997.

Powell, Jillian. *Wind and Us.* Mankato, Minn.: Smart Apple Media, 1999.

Internet Sites

Eduscapes Online Topics
http://www.eduscapes.com/42explore/wind.htm

National Oceanic and Atmospheric Association (NOAA) Research
http://www.oar.noaa.gov/k12

The Franklin Institute Science Museum Online
http://www.fi.edu/weather/index.html

Weather Safety with Owlie Skywarn, National Weather Service Mascot
http://www.crh.noaa.gov/mkx/owlie/owlie.htm

INFORMATION